W9-CEO-847

THE •UNABRIDGED, •UNCENSORED, •UNBELIEVABLE Garfield®

BY: JIM DAVIS

BALLANTINE BOOKS • NEW YORK

Copyright © 1986 by United Feature Syndicate, Inc.

All rights reserved under International and Pan-American Copyright Conventions. Published in the United States by Ballantine Books, a division of Random House, Inc., New York, and simultaneously in Canada by Random House of Canada Limited, Toronto.

Library of Congress Catalog Card Number: 86-90729

ISBN: 0-345-33772-7

Manufactured in the United States of America

First Edition: November 1986

10 9 8 7 6 5 4 3 2 1

CLAWED CAT
I SHRED YOUR HIDE. I STEP ON YOUR FACE

DECLAWED CAT
SPARE ME! I'M TOO GOOD-LOOKING TO DIE!

HOW CATS APPEAR TO GET INTO HIGH PLACES...

UNFAIR TO CATS
KNOCK OVER THE CAT

HAPPY CAT'S TAIL
SAD CAT'S TAIL
ANGRY CAT'S TAIL
ENTERTAINING CAT'S TAIL
SOME ENCHANTED EVENING

CAT NIGHTMARE #496
SNIFF SNIFF

SUSHI

WORMS

CAT NIGHTMARE #32

IN SPORTS NEWS... CAT SEASON OPENS TODAY

LONG JOHN CATLOVER

SLURP!

GARFIELD'S TAG TEAM PARTNER THINKS FAST
ANN

BUG
BOMB

RESPONSIBLE CAT
WHAP!
SQUEEK

IRRESPONSIBLE CAT
HERE, BOZO. HOLD MY HAT WHILE I EAT THIS CHEESE
WHATEVER

SLIPPERY
WHEN
WET

12

POOR ME. STUCK ON A DESERT ISLAND WITH NOTHING TO EAT
Z

CAUTIO
LOW-
FLYING
SLEIGHS

BOING

CAT NIGHTMARE #426
NEWS
DOGS GIVEN VOTE

I DON'T LIKE THE LOOK OF THIS, ODIE

I'M JUST GOING "TRICKING" TONIGHT
SOAP

WALK THAT CAT FOR YOU, MISTER?
CAT WALKING SERVICE

HUMANS

EEEEEEK!

MAD DOG!
MAD DOG!

WHY CATS DON'T DRIVE TRUCKS
NO! NO! TO THE LEFT! THE LEFT!
EMER
FUEL
H
C
F
R

I'LL HAVE THE SAUMON FUMÉ AND MY DOG WILL HAVE THE ROAD KILL DU JOUR

KITTY LITTER
TRASH

GARFIELD WITH SHADES

GARFIELD WITH MINI BLINDS

ONE OF THE DANGERS OF
OVER-PETTING YOUR CAT

CATS OF THE WORLD
GERMANY
FRANCE
MEXICO
CANADA

munch munch ERP!
AKES
FREE GERBAL INSIDE!

SOMETHING ABOUT THIS PLACE GIVES ME THE CREEPS

MAILMAN CHART
SHOULDER
PRIME RIB
RUMP ROAST
THIGH
LEG
MANY PARTS OF A MAILMAN ARE EDIBLE

IT SEEMS LIKE EVERY TIME WE MAKE A MOVE, THE CATS ARE WAITING FOR US! NOW I WANNA KNOW WHY?!
MATCHES

COWARDLY DOG RUNNING AWAY FROM HIS TAIL

ODIE AT BIRTH

WHAT DOGS TALK ABOUT:
I SAY THIS THING ABOUT TURNING AROUND THREE TIMES TO LIE DOWN IS OVERRATED. I TURN AROUND TWICE AND FIND MY PLACE JUST FINE
IT CAN BE OVERDONE TOO. MY COUSIN ONCE TURNED AROUND FOUR TIMES... GOT DIZZY, AND FELL OFF THE FRONT PORCH

ANCIENT EGYPTIAN MODE OF TRANSPORTATION FOR CATS:

MILK

CAT ON A HOT FUDGE SUNDAE:

CHEAP CAT TOUPEE:

NOUVEAU RICHE CATS:
ROVER! YOU'RE DROOLING IN THE CANAPÉS AGAIN!
IT'S SO HARD TO FIND GOOD HELP THESE DAYS
SO I SAID TO IRMA, "WE CAN AFFORD IT. GO AHEAD AND GET THE ELECTRIC FUR LICKER"
I'D LOOK THAT GOOD TOO IF I HAD MY EARS BOBBED AS MANY TIMES AS SHE HAS

EXCUSE ME, SIR. ARE YOU BY ANY CHANCE A CAT OWNER?
WHY, YES I AM. HOW DID YOU KNOW?

THE CAT THAT INSPIRED...
"CATS ALWAYS LAND ON THEIR FEET"

CATS HAVING FUN ON A WAXED TABLE

A DOG TO AVOID

CRASH!
THUP!

STALKING THE WILD LEAF

CAT NIGHTMARE #11

OKAY, GUYS. WE GOTTA TAKE THIS CLOCK BY ONE!

CAT NIGHTMARE #47
scrit!

SHECKY CAT PLAYS TO A TOUGH HOUSE:
I KNEW A DOG WHO WAS SO STUPID, CARS CHASED HIM!
BOO!
HISS!
GRRR
GET HIM OUTTA HERE!
BOO!

SPAT!

SIAMESE CATS:

NERMAL
WORLDS CUTEST CAT
TA-DA!
LOTION
Facial Cream
Fume

CAT CLAIMING ITS TERRITORY

DOGS... APPLY WITHIN
BEWARE OF DOG
TRESPASSERS WILL BE LICKED
ENTER AT YOUR OWN RISK

THINGS CATS SHOULDN'T SHARPEN THEIR CLAWS ON:

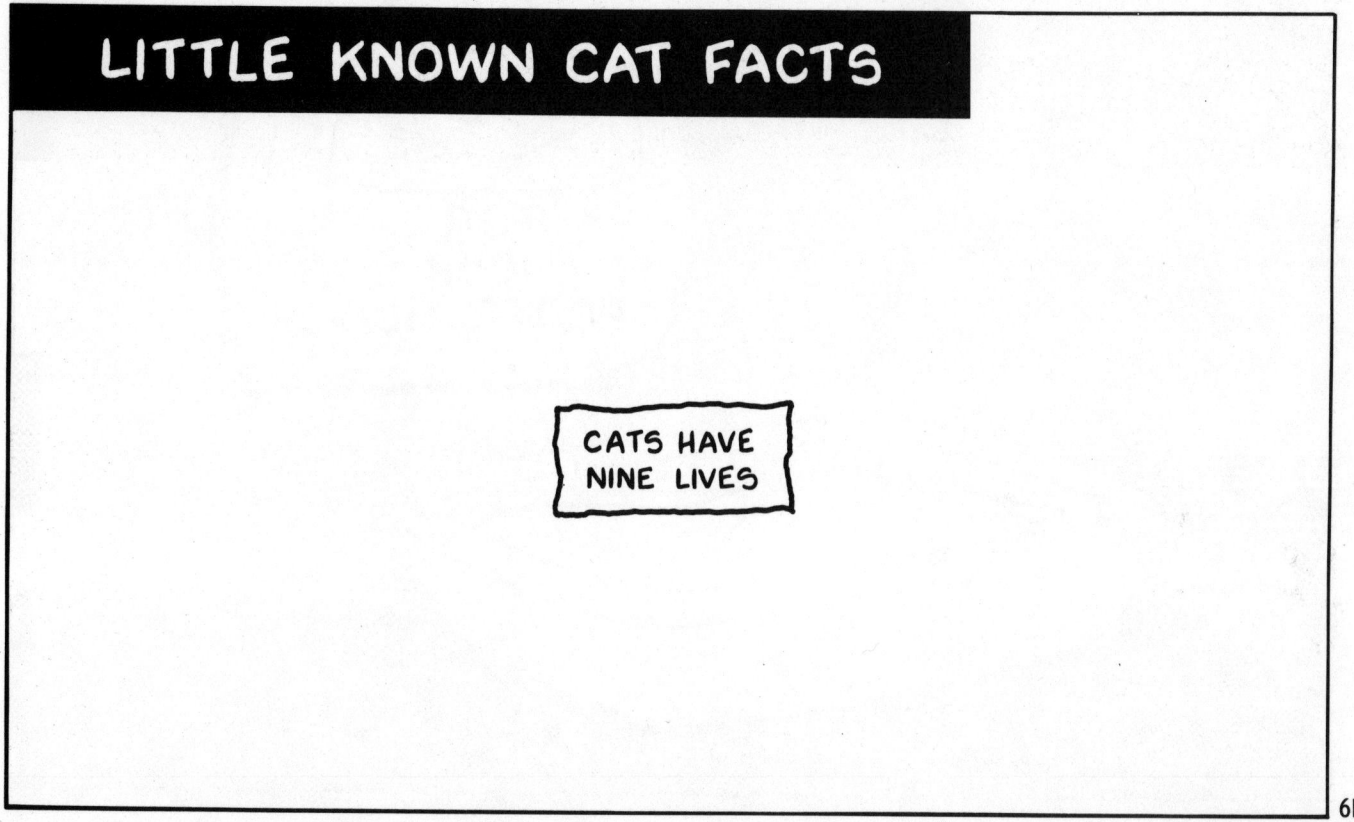
LITTLE KNOWN CAT FACTS
CATS HAVE NINE LIVES

FOR
YOUR
PROTECTION

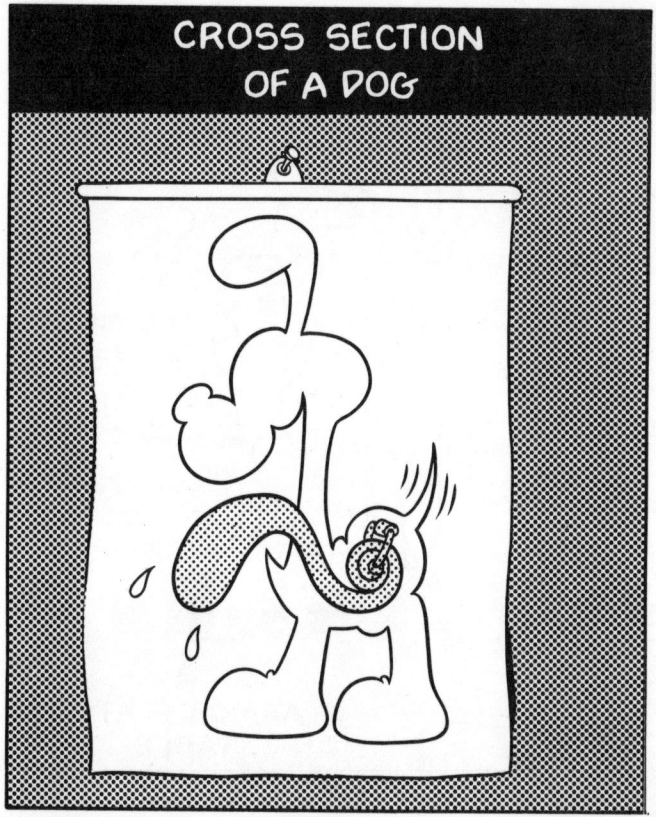
CROSS SECTION
OF A DOG

CORNDOG

FURNITURE FOR CAT OWNERS
PLASTIC FLOWERS
CHAIN MAIL CURTAINS
ALUMINUM VASE
STAINLESS STEEL COUCH
LUCITE THROW RUG
ARMOR PLATED TABLE